You are a Success !

Mary Robinson

HEART PUBLISHING & PRODUCTIONS
Portland, Oregon

61 Proven Strategies for Developing SUCCESS

Library of Congress Catalog Number: 90-085787
ISBN : 0-9628496-4-2

First printing, April 1991

Published & distributed in the United States by

HEART PUBLISHING & PRODUCTIONS
PO Box 82037
Portland, OR 97282 USA

Dedication

I DEDICATE THIS BOOK TO MY son, Brynie James Robinson. A child's love endures all things, it seems. Brynie has loved me during the challenging as well as the rewarding times. He depends on me to be his mom and has only needed me to be O.K. with myself. When you're caught in a cycle where there appears to be no way out, the healing powers of a child's embrace are amazing.

Brynie is a child full of light, love and magic. His presence and love have consistently motivated me to move up and off the spiraling cycles of mistaken perception. With each breakthrough, we both were able to enjoy more peace, love and comfort within our relationship.

Brynie's unconditional love, regard and acceptance gave me the courage to discipline myself and to climb back up and dust myself off. He has been the light of my life in the darkest of moments. My desire to be a positive influence and role model for him has been the driving force in creating a loving and successful existence. My love for him is eternal and I thank God each and every day that he is in my life.

Mom,
even when we both argue,
we're both right!
　　　–BRYNIE JAMES ROBINSON, AGE 5

Acknowledgments

I acknowledge with appreciation and love:
My many students, clients, friends and family who have supported me in putting my ideas into a program and book.

Fran Strom for her friendship and exciting creativity which includes the lay-out, design and beautiful art work of this book. Christi Payne for saying this was fun and for her design and typesetting capabilities.

My friends and typesetters, Jim Sleeper and Melody Englund, for helping me rush the contents of this book into its prototype printing.

To my editors: my sister Markreta (Sam) Brandt; my friends, Chris Arb, Sharon Cannon, Judy Cooper, Vincent Samatowic, Gretchen Sperling and Berdell Moffett; Thea Rhiannon and Sandy Ryan who have all taught me much during the editing process and helped keep the positive intent of this book consistent and inviting; Casey Chaney for coaching me in the editing of the introduction to express the messages from my heart with clarity.

Great Quotations, Inc. for the many quotes I used from their booklet, *The Best of Success*.

My aunt Janet Turner, for diligently researching the authors of the quotes I chose to use in this book. My aunt Musa Brown, who sent me her quotes from the cookbook she's used for seventy years. As she cooked, she would have certain quotes come to mind. She'd quickly write them down and now after all these years, they were there for me to use. And to my aunt LaVerne Bish, for hearing the message of my book and sending me some material I could use.

Julian Goble for the way he captured the essence of success in the photographs of my son and me.

John West, Jim Lekas, Connie Dawson, Dan Grimes, Ron Munkres, Sandy Howell and Robby Robinson for supporting me in the beginning when I was developing the strategies in this book.

My parents for loving me and providing support and encouragement in all my endeavors.

A special thanks to Mary and Haven Boggs for ministering to me and thousands of other's who are rediscovering their relationship to themselves and to God.

Craig Reynolds for his love, vision and commitment through the final stages of completing this book.

I love you all. From my heart to your hearts, God Bless.

Introduction

T HIS BOOK IS ABOUT *PERSPECTIVE* AS IT RELATES
to success. Everybody perceives success differently.
Some see it as financial abundance, career fulfillment, peace
of mind, physical well being, healthy loving relationships
and more. Our definitions of success may shift as we grow
and change through different periods of our lives. The form
of success I once strived to aquire, personally and profes-
sionally, almost cost me my life. My perception of success
needed to be strengthened and realigned with purpose and
intent.

One of my favorite illustrations of perspective is the
example of Babe Ruth. The year he had the most home runs
was also the year he had the most strike outs. The idea of
perspective which underlies this story has helped me to pick
myself up and brush myself off time and time again when
I faced the pain of what appeared to be failure. As a result
of practicing positive perspective, I have come to expect an
abundance of success to be a part of my daily experience.

Whether our perspective is positive or negative is
always a matter of choice. It often appears that we are
victims without choice; we are not. It is our choice to keep
swinging even though we have struck out. That doesn't
mean we don't take a moment to breathe between times up

at bat. I reached a point in my life where it was necessary to go sit on the bench and give it a rest. I had been trying too hard to be successful on too many levels.

*"No matter how simple
or how difficult the choice....
It always comes back to,
'It is your choice.'"*

In 1984, during the early stages of labor, the placenta ripped away from my uterus, causing immediate death to our unborn child. My husband and I were devastated. Because our baby was otherwise perfect, I felt like an absolute failure as a woman and as a mother. When, nine months later, I became pregnant again, I was terrorized at the possiblity of losing another child. It was an emotionally distressing time for me. I experienced anger, sadness and exhaustion, projecting the worst possible scenario, while still attempting to be hopeful. My husband expressed his anxiety and fear by withdrawing emotionally and physically from our relationship. Neither of us had resolved the conflict and guilt over the death of our first son. We didn't know how to at the time.

With my stress level up, I was hospitalized five times for premature labor. As soon as my doctor had determined the lungs were fully developed, he delivered our baby by C-Section in order to avoid any birth complications. Despite the successful arrival of a healthy baby boy, I continued to feel like a failure. I believed, rather perceived, it was my body that had failed our first son. I felt certain I would bear this burdon for eternity.

While living with this pain and confusion, Brynie was spitting up most of what he ate. After taking him to medical specialists and having several series of tests run and a gastrointestinal examination performed, we found that there was nothing physically wrong with him. Because of my background in psychology, I understood all too clearly that Brynie's problem was a symptom of the disharmony in our marriage.

My unhappiness in the marriage coupled with the results of these tests helped me realize my husband and I needed to separate. It was mutually agreed upon that Brynie would reside with me. Shortly thereafter, he stopped spitting up. Though my husband and I loved each other deeply, we didn't have the energy or the tools to bring our marriage back together. We sadly divorced less than one year after Brynie was born.

The emotional pain and the headaches that I had carried with me since childhood now escalated. I had been using Fiorinal (aspirin, compounded with a barbiturate called Butabital to relieve anxiety) since I was 19. Now my doctor was prescribing enough for me to be taking 8-10 tablets a day. I considered my life a failure, with the exception of Brynie.

Another reason for my perception of failure was that I believed my success was dependent upon other people needing me. I had spent my life up to this point trying to become what I thought other people needed me to be. Now, after the loss of my firstborn son, a high-risk pregnancy, a new baby and a divorce, I was overwhelmed. My work was beginning to show symptoms of burnout. At the time, I was a high school counselor. I loved my work and in the past I had enjoyed high levels of success with all types of students, especially the kids at risk. I was determined to survive the school year but now I struggled every step of the way to enjoy any form of the success I was still capable of producing with my students.

An opportunity to move to Oregon came to me, and I decided that a move would be good for me. I finished the year and moved. After settling into my new home, I found myself exhausted emotionally and physically. How could so much tragedy have happened to me in such a short amount of time? What was I doing wrong? These questions, and more, filled my head and my world as I began to read, study and search for the meaning of life.

I just wanted to be a wife and mother. I just wanted to matter to someone. As a little girl, I didn't think I ever wanted to be a professional at anything, yet I was good at what I did, so I did it because I thought I was supposed to. This was not really what I had wanted. However, everything I did, I did because I thought I was supposed to. I was encouraged not to question established norms or move against the grain; especially not to put my own well-being first. This was not the way it was in my favorite fairy tale.

I had attempted self-exploration several times before in my life. I would start reading and studying psychology and religion. Then, I'd start feeling better and my self-esteem would radiate from me and I'd get myself into a new relationship. The last time that happened, I got married. This time, I couldn't even consider the idea of marriage. I knew I had my work cut out for me. The emotional and physical pain I was in was too severe for me to ignore.

As a result of my research, I once again started

remembering who I was at many different levels: physical, mental, emotional and spiritual. In reconnecting with my spiritual source, I was reminded of the simple Sunday school principles I learned as a child – principles such as, "Do unto others as you would have them do unto you," and "Love thy neighbor as thyself." I had utilized these same principles as a professional, often without realizing it. Now, as I recalled some of these simple lessons, I reapplied them to my personal life. Little by little, I began experiencing success. I began feeling better and wanting more for myself.

After nine months of getting my feet back on the ground physically, emotionally and spiritually, I realized I needed to end my relationship with the Fiorinal. After all, it was a mood-altering drug. I knew it was contributing to my inability to experience myself fully and naturally.

It took me thirteen days to detoxify safely in a hospital. Afterward, I immediately went into an outpatient drug treatment program for women. There, I worked steadily on the core of all my addictions...my inability to love myself.

In learning how to love myself, I needed to feel my own inner success. How was I to do this? I've heard it said that we teach what we most need to learn. Amazingly true for my life!

Success! yes, yes, yes!

A S A HIGH SCHOOL CHEERLEADER, ONE OF MY favorite cheers was:

"S-U-C-C-E-S-S, THAT'S THE WAY
TO SPELL SUCCESS!!"

Corny, I know, but if we could only keep this cheer resonating in our heads, we'd increase our potential considerably. Realize that the intent of this cheer was to affirm that success was at hand.

In my work with "the kids nobody wants," I found that when I refused to see their failures as failure, it lightened their load as well as mine. Let's say a child is coloring outside the lines. Instead of focusing on the lines, I will attend to the fact that he is accomplishing the task. I will praise his efforts. After all, it is an issue of developmental ability and coordination, not failure. It is more important that the child want to continue to practice. He will get it eventually if the heart of the child's efforts is acknowledged. This replaces all nagging about apparent failure, thus developing a consciousness of success. Granted, at times, I can only find a smidgen, but I make the itty-bitty successes apparent to the child. The result is an immediate, if not total, turnaround in the way he performs in my classroom. This also applies to forthcoming situations where he may find himself dealing with a perception of failure.

What works for children works for adults. The depth of my work in this area came from assisting other adults who work with children, helping them learn to get in touch with the childlike part of themselves that needs to be more fully alive, expressed and nurtured. Over the years, I found that children have a greater likelihood of success when we have adults working with them who can experience and embrace childlike perception. These adults have a greater sensitivity to what has to happen to assist a child in experiencing inner and outer success. By the same token, the adult who works on bridging issues of the past to circumstances of the present, will also be developing his or her own success.

Children teach us exactly what we need to know. Their failures are our failures. Their success is our success. Research is indicating that we are what we are because of deep-seated beliefs that were established from our childhood perceptions of our experiences. Each of us still feels our own childhood experiences at a very deep emotional and sometimes physical level. Often, it seems that we've been trying to separate ourselves from our childhood just because we became adults, or maybe it's because our childhood was too painful. Being an adult, acting like an adult changes nothing. There is and always will be a child within each and every one of us who needs to be consoled and nurtured to some degree. Listening to that child within helps us maintain our self-esteem and aids in our development of even higher levels of awareness and experiences of personal success.

Research also shows that in our present addiction-based society, the base of many addictions is inadequate and/or painful childhood experiences. If, as children, we perceived ourselves as being less than what we were inherently meant to be, we feel as if we are lacking something as adults. This negative core belief causes separation of self, and separation of self decreases self-esteem.

This legacy of believing we are less than what we can be has to stop in order for our children to survive the state of confusion and separation present in our society today. It begins with us, the adults. Success automatically has a ripple effect on what we love and cherish. In learning how to establish our own levels of success, we will have an impact on the success of our families, community and all of society.

Addictions come about through our attempts to fill our fear of lack of self. In my case, the headaches I'd suffered since the age of four were an indication of my own self-invalidation. The pain was only heightened by stress, which constricted my body in such a way that compressed the flow of blood through my neck and shoulder area. As a result, I had a 17-year use of prescription medicine. The stress for me was a fairly constant fear of failure; a fear that was ever present within me at a very deep level.

Because of my background in educational psychology and family therapy, I knew that whatever pain, confusion and sense of separation I didn't resolve would pass on to my son. In my recovery and healing work, I constantly applied those principles and strategies I'd rediscovered, methods that I knew worked because I had used them for years with at-risk youth and adults in crisis. Now it was finally time for me to bridge what I knew worked from my professional experience into my personal existence.

In doing so, I learned that inner success comes about in myriad ways. One may be financial. How we are doing financially can be a direct reflection of how we are doing in our relationships and in our physical and emotional well-being. Inner success may also come from our contributions to society as well as taking care of ourselves. Success for you may be as simple as learning how to give of yourself in ways that increase your energy, not deplete it. This means giving for giving's sake, without expecting a return. The result of this attitude is a greater return than you might have expected, creating more energy.

For me, success has been learning over and over how to take care of myself and realizing how I can experience myself as fully alive when I'm unconditionally loving and giving.

Success comes through the development of the mind and through the determination and willingness to shift our perceptions. And yes, sometimes it takes pain, separation and confusion before we become willing to look at things from a different perspective.

I learned that success does not come from overextending myself and working excessive hours for outside approval. It comes from an inner love of self and feeling of purpose and direction. If I feel I don't have a purpose or am not receiving any direction, then it's time for me to slow down and allow my purpose to evolve into my consciousness. The same may be true for you. You may find that success is not how much you do, but how much of what you do contributes to what you love and to those you love. As you'll discover, success involves much more than the constant approval of others. It may also include a spiritual center as your base, approval of yourself, care and nurturance of your home and family, your work and your community.

Developing success is the key component to healthy, satisfying relationships at work, home or play. Experiencing the development of success often involves adjusting perspective, whether it be related to issues with children, adolescents or adults. It is about how we can turn our experience of failure or loss into one of success and freedom.

> *Success frees us to experience*
>   *love of self*
>   *love of family*
>   *love of community*
>   *and love of all humanity....*

Breaking the cycles of failure

*G*ETTING TO SUCCESS MEANS BREAKING through our experiences of failure. In order to aquire success in all areas of our lives, we must first shift our perceptions of failure. We must see the patterns of behavior we have established that bring us experiences of being less than who we are. Failure is nothing more than a picture of how we continually "get in our own way!" It is an illustration of what we believe has to be the truth for us.

We may be the most successful people in the world, yet if we have one person resist our help, we may feel some degree of failure. In these situations, it seems it doesn't matter how hard we try to get this person to like us, respect us, treat us right or even acknowledge our fine, fine efforts. Of course, we can say that it is just that person, i.e., "Everybody knows how difficult George is to work with." But somehow, deep inside, there is a "knowing" that keeps pulling at us to figure out why George doesn't respond. Something tells us that it has something to do with us. Could we possibly have a cycle of failure within us that's rearing its ugly head?

Of course we could. We're human, after all. And George is establishing a cycle of failure with us, also, when we allow ourselves to participate with him in this fashion.

Breaking cycles of failure means not supporting failure as the only means of attention. A strong reaction to a negative reinforces more of the same.

I once had a young college student living with me who was recovering from addiction to alcohol and other substances. She had a history of being a victim. It became apparent to me early that the topic of most of our conversations was about how other people were constantly mistreating her. Getting her to be accountable for her participation as a victim took some time and work. The challenge for me was to focus her attention on those things she did well and could figure out for herself. I stretched myself to make conscientious decisions to reduce, if not eliminate, my reactions to anything negative in her behavior. When she needed more attention than I was willing to give, she would go out and increase the level of failure she was experiencing, then drop hints to me around the house. My biggest lesson was to learn not to react to the failure. The way to do this is embodied in the 61 proven strategies.

Often, people fail as an expression of anger or resentment or as a way of asking for help and support. If you listen as people talk about how they are failing in relationships, work and life in general, you will soon discover there is a cyclic effect. There are those people who are striving to get it figured out and there are those people who just seem to go around and around and around. Sometimes, it takes going around enough times before one becomes fed up with the way things are spiraling downward. This anger, frustration, pain or confusion may be the very thing a person needs to break free of a cycle of failure.

To break your own cycle means to move off it by replacing your "failure talk" with "success talk." What have you succeeded in? Notice the difference in the audience you begin to attract. Perhaps you have a group of friends who seem to have nothing but problems. Yet, when you change what *you* talk about, you may notice you start to attract people who are experiencing success. They view life as some sort of fun treat! We seem to find whatever we are looking for.

Making new truths for yourself creates new perceptions. You'll find that you'll want to be a part of the solution not the problem. New perceptions enhance and nurture self-esteem. Self-esteem gives you the gumption to get out there and see yourself as capable and competent in all that you attempt to do. Every attempt has within it an element or seed of success. Even when it's challenging to find what that is, find it. Build upon it, use it, stretch it and you will be breaking a cycle, a mistaken belief about what you once believed was your only reality.

AN ONGOING PROCESS

This book came about as a wonderful surprise to me, my family and my friends. I had been working on what I thought was going to be my first book, *Breaking the Cycles of Failure/Healing Today's Children*. It was based on a success-orientated program that I had developed and had worked long and hard to integrate and practice for myself. I gradually discovered I was making breakthrough after breakthrough in my own personal experience of success. I understood that the working title I'd chosen for my book was relatively long, but I couldn't seem to split the title until the eve of my birthday.

That evening, I visualized the two titles separating, and I understood that I was really trying to write two books at once. The next day I attended a consulting workshop to learn more about promoting myself as a motivational speaker and consultant. As an example, the speaker, Paul Franklin, used a promotional booklet about strategies for repeat consulting business. I realized immediately that I had at least 50 strategies for breaking cycles of failure. Could I write a book on these strategies? Yes, yes, yes! I missed the entire next hour of the workshop as my ideas came streaming forth...and why wouldn't they? These were the very things I'd been teaching and practicing for years.

I showed my final draft of *Breaking the Cycles of Failure* to my friends and asked for their quick feedback. Shortly before the book was to go to print, a good supportive friend, Vincent, called and said he felt the title was too negative. From what he could tell, he said, this book was really about success, not failure.

I resisted his input at first, then realized that he was absolutely right. I changed the title immediately. I felt the change from failure to success at an incredibly deep level. For the first time, I experienced my own shift away from having to break any more cycles of failure, or what I had determined to be failure, to a new awareness of myself as someone who demonstrates success.

It was only an issue of perception, my own perception. Remember, failure is an illustration of what we believe has to be true. From the moment I retitled this book to success,

I too, accepted my success, at long last. I realized how, over the past seven years, I've broken cycle after cycle of my perceptions of myself as a failure. To break cycles of failure, it is necessary to: one, be accountable for yourself and, two, take the smidgens of truth that are positive about your nature and stretch them for all they are worth. Through increasing your focus on the positive aspects of your nature, you will become more and more of that which you desire to be.

What we have done
will not be lost to all eternity.
Everything ripens
at its time,
and becomes fruit
at its hour.

—ROSANNE SANDERS

Developing Success

MIKE GOODMAN'S BOOK, *HOW TO WIN,* popularized a method of increasing the size of the next bet after a win using this formula—1-2-3-5; this calls for an initial bet of one unit and a bet on one unit after every loss. After a win, the size of the bet is increased to two units. After the second win, to three units, after the third win, to five units. After two wins, all invested funds in the series are house money, and each win thereafter shows a nice profit. Goodman recommends 1-2-3-5 and then remaining at five once this level is reached. This could very well be extended to 1-2-3-5-8-12-etc., depending on individual preference.

Developing success means focusing less on loss and more on parlaying already existing success. Progressing when winning uses the parlay principle of increasing the size of a wager with profits. While I don't gamble with cards, I do like to increase the profits of my success. With each experience of success, I feel more confident in utilizing a strategy to develop even higher levels of success.

What I like about the 1-2-3-5 formula is that you still bet one unit after every loss. Because I know the strategies I've developed work, if I experience anything less than success when implementing one of them, I will still bet on the strategy (one unit) until I experience success two times in a row. After two experiences of success with a new strategy, I consider myself "in the black" or making a profit.

Now, developing success is not about betting, even though it can entail taking some educated risks. It's about perspective and taking a chance on what you already know works. It's about taking methods that have worked for you in the past, and using them with more consistency, discipline and fortitude. It takes time, for it is a process that increases as you increase your willingness to persevere with what you know works when you work it.

Giving in to negativity may cause you to take a couple of steps back, and that's par for the course. This is a necessary step in developing trust and confidence with anything new or contrary to previous experience.

In comparison to what you once experienced in your life, success can often feel awkward or too good to be true. Because of this, you may fail at something in an attempt to hang on to the past or the familar. You may deter yourself in order to support an old belief that, "I don't deserve to have it this good." Be willing to go nose-to-nose with that belief. Be firm and persistent with it until it gives way to your new perceptions of success, and then release it to the ethers of the universe. Bid it farewell and get on with enjoying the success you now deserve.

So you see, failure isn't really failure after all. It's just a picture that needs to be retouched.

Success takes some getting used to, so give yourself a break, and rack up all the successes you've already had and parlay them into your present experience.

HOW TO USE THIS BOOK

This book is intended for a diverse audience, including educators, parents, helping professionals and employers. It is for any person who desires to develop or increase his or her personal experience with success. The strategies you will learn here are the ones I have gathered over a period of 15 years in personal growth work and professional experience with numerous youth and adults in crisis.

You don't have to have a child in your life to utilize the strategies here. The methods I've gathered simply support all human endeavor. They have been tested and proven with children from age 1 to 91. They work, regardless of your childhood experience, and will provide a firm foundation as you develop the levels of success you desire.

These 61 strategies have saved my life and they offer

me success every time I remember to utilize what I know. They are reminders to me that I can approve of myself and that I need to get in touch with my feelings and honor what is going on inside of me. Sometimes they remind me to address that inner voice. These strategies work, and because they work, I have put my faith and trust in them in developing my ongoing personal success.

Beside each strategy, you will find a quote from a well-known person who has practiced and possibly still is practicing success. Each quote will connect you to the simplicity of the strategy, thus motivating and inspiring you to stretch yourself, to reach out for all that life has to offer.

These strategies work. They assist you in staying focused in the face of confusion and conflict. They help you discover what's not working and where you are in relationship to the situation. They will help you clear the way to opening new lines of communication and levels of agreement.

They are principles to live by because they always work, when you work them. There are many familiar themes here. It is an issue of how willing you are to practice them and allow them to be integrated into your life. Utilize the strategies as a guide to assist you and those you love in living life fully and confidently.

Remember, failure is merely an example of how we lock our hearts and minds away and attach ourselves to the idea that there is only one road to take in our lives. Success shows us a variety of roads, and that is the beauty of these 61 strategies. You can open this book anywhere and find a strategy that's meant just for you and your situation.

If a man has a talent and cannot use it, he has failed. If he has a talent and uses only half of it, he has partly failed. If he has a talent and learns somehow to use the whole of it, he has gloriously succeeded, and won a satisfaction and a triumph few men ever know.

—THOMAS WOLFE

From my heart to your heart

This is a book of celebration. All too often, people working through their problems or addictions forget to stop and smell the roses. This is a book about success right here and right now. The past simply does not matter once you understand that you are the master of your own success.

This book is designed to remind you that you already are a success. It is your gift to all humanity at a time when this kind of individualized display of courage and fortitude is needed to heal our children and the ills of our society. And it is happening and will continue to happen as long as we all become accountable to that which is inherently ours to be and to give.

So, go ahead, *make the shift and retouch your life with success*. Then pass it on and on and on.

Take heart in your attempts to be all that you want to be. Know that you have what it takes to touch up the pictures of the past into any magnificent work of art that you find yourself being pulled to create within you. That pull is what you are here to do.

And please know, *YOU ARE A SUCCESS!*

Peace, love and light
be with you on your road
in developing personal freedom, fulfillment,
and success

Mary Robinson

Success

He has achieved success who
has lived well
Laughed often,
 and loved much;
Who has gained the respect of
intelligent men,
And the love of little children;
Who has filled his niche and
accomplished his task;
Who has left the world better
than he found it,
Whether by an improved poppy,
a perfect poem,
Or a rescued soul;
Who has always looked for the
best in others
And given the best he had;
Whose life was an inspiration;
Whose memory a benediction.

–B.A. Stanley

Keep it simple and meaningful

These 61 strategies will help you determine what needs to happen to develop your own inner success. They are gentle reminders that help resolve conflict and pain. Remember, failure is only an illustration of what you believe has to be the truth. You can do whatever you choose to do with this picture. Each strategy encourages you to acknowledge and honor the various aspects of your nature; to be who you are, to give yourself a break and to allow love, light and peace to be your daily experience.

The artwork on the following pages are selected pieces of the book's cover. Each piece has within it the potential for individual interpretation and meaning. As with the strategies, each picture has an image representing an aspect of the whole. The intention of the artwork is to suggest the kind of beauty and simplicity which is ever present within each of us when we look to ourselves for success.

If there's a way to do it better . . .
find it.

—Thomas A. Edison

1. Observe yourself!

S TEP ASIDE. CHECK YOURSELF out. If you find that you are trying to get other people to support something that you've done or to support you because of something that you feel has happened to you, observe yourself. Are you feeling guilty in some way? Are you feeling violated? Up to this point, your perspective is coming from a place inside you where there could be a past hurt. Look for it.

If, from an observer's position, you can see that this situation is not as intense as you experienced it, then something is presenting itself for you to look at and resolve. Pretend you are watching yourself on television. How are you participating in this situation? Observing yourself is a great self-correcting strategy. It can get you out of the victim position and back in the driver's seat. You may quickly adjust your manner and tone.

Sometimes it's not always easy or delightful to see yourself as you really are. Be gentle with yourself and know it's just an issue of fine-tuning. It can be very healing to know that you *can* be in charge of how you are viewed by people who matter to you. Self-observation is a matter of perspective, *yours*. It elevates self-concept and self-esteem to observe yourself correcting a situation successfully.

Observing yourself can also help you become better focused and emotionally available to the people you are interacting with. Being fully present allows you a more in-depth understanding of yourself and what pushes your buttons. From an observer's position, you can immediately see the solution and determine how to deal more effectively with this and similar situations in the future. Getting a clear picture from an outside position increases the probability of success.

Reflect upon your present blessings,
of which every man has many;
not on your past misfortunes,
of which all men have some.
　　　　　　　　—CHARLES DICKENS

2. Get amnesia.

IT HAS BEEN SAID THAT WE ARE products of our pasts. And while this is true, we often let our focus *take root* in the negative aspects of someone's nature without even giving them a chance to get up to bat. How many times have we refused to give someone a chance because we've heard about their past before we have even met them? Sometimes we meet them, like them and then find out about their past. If their past was negative in some way we may abandon any form of a relationship without taking any more time to know them.

Getting amnesia stops the attraction to the negative immediately and allows you to remain in a position of unconditional regard and acceptance. You don't have to know someone's past to treat them with human regard. In fact, it's best that you don't know their past until you've had a chance to experience them for a period of time, thus making and trusting your own observations and feelings.

When first meeting someone, we may ask them how many times they've been married, how many children they have, and what, exactly, they've done for a living up until now. We tend to hold onto the past as if it protects us *from them* in some way. Oddly enough, the opposite frequently happens. We want to prepare ourselves to avoid the worst. We believe that if we just remind them of their past often enough and in *diplomatic* ways, they will not ever do, whatever "it" is again! Should work, right?

What do these constant reminders bring? Most likely, a repeat of the past, because we aren't envisioning anything new, different or better. Chances are, even if they did do something new, we'd probably miss it because our focus would be on remembering the past.

What if we knew nothing about each others' pasts? Getting amnesia allows us to be fully present and accountable for ourselves and our actions. Getting amnesia encourages speaking to situations directly and as they occur instead of expecting the worst and assuming we already know the answers for someone else.

You have already survived the past. Why allow it to hurt you or others further?

The freedom to fail is vital
if you're going to succeed.
Most successful men fail time and time again,
and it is a measure of the strength
that failure merely propels them
into some new attempt at success.

—Michael Korda

3. Allow people their lessons.

OFTEN, WE TRY TO CARRY SOMEONE else's pain. Why? Because we genuinely care. It is rough to see someone you care for going through a difficult time. Yet you can be supportive, loving, and nurturing and still allow people to do what they need to do. (Sometimes, their experience is a lesson for us as well.)

We may have to go so far as to intervene to save someone's life. But beyond getting a person to safety, we must allow each person to do his own healing.

The analogy I often think of is a wounded animal. An injured animal will hide itself in the brush and lick its wounds. If another like and loving animal of the forest comes along and sees its brother hurting, it will lay down quietly and wait for it to rest and heal. As the injured animal feels better, the helping animal will go and get food. Healing comes from moral support and physical closeness.

This may be all you need to do for a person who is struggling with pain. Be *PATIENT*. Allow that person to heal himself from within. It will ultimately be his source of strength.

You can have anything you want—
if you want it badly enough.
You can be anything you want to be,
have anything you desire,
accomplish anything you set out to accomplish—
if you will hold to that desire
with singleness of purpose . . .

—ROBERT COLLIER

4. Reverse the negatives... affirm something new.

BEHAVIOR IS AN ILLUSION. Behavior is a picture a person paints of what it is he believes to be the truth about himself. Every one of us has within us the potential to be, do and have what our hearts desire. We must be willing to do whatever it takes to make this happen. We must see ourselves in a different way and affirm what we want this to look like.

Reverse the negative aspects of yourself in the picture you want to create. Affirm the reverse of what *appears* to be the truth about yourself right now. If your original picture portrayed you as rebellious, lazy and good-for-nothing, the reverse would be agreeable, active and worthwhile.

Reversing allows your mind to see other possibilities and to develop new ideas about yourself. Reversing and re-affirming is not magic; it just feels that way. You will notice a shift as you begin to experience yourself with your new affirmations.

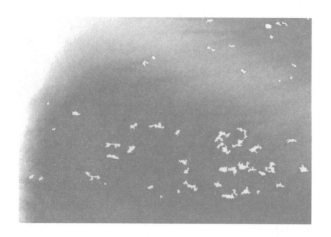

You learn that, whatever you are doing in life,
obstacles don't matter very much.
Pain or other circumstances can be there,
but if you want to do a job bad enough,
you'll find a way to get it done.

—JACK YOUNGBLOOD

5. Do something different.

*I*NSANITY IS DOING THE SAME THING *over and over again and expecting different results*. Seriously, if something is not working, it's not working. It could be that you're trying too hard to force the other person to "get it," when the only person who needs to get it is you.

This may seem a bit overwhelming at first, but trust that if you don't like the situation you are in, then it is you who must be accountable for your own well-being. This isn't always easy, yet it is this simple. Enlisting the support of others may or may not help. Attempting something different is at least worth a try. Integrity in all attempts will enhance your chances at breaking an existing cycle in which the outcome appears to be less than success.

Once you've decided what it is you want to do differently, see yourself doing it, affirm that you already are doing it, act "as if" you already know how to do it, and then, when the opportunity presents itself to you, *do it*.

Wisdom is knowing what to do next,
Skill is knowing how to do it,
And virtue is doing it.

—DAVID STARR JORDAN

6. Sit on yourself.

REGULATING MY WEIGHT IS SOMETHING I "know" how to do. Doing what is necessary to maintain a weight that is comfortable for me is another issue! Sometimes, it's easy to turn away from eating more than I need to feel full. Other times, it's as if I'm driven beyond reason. It's at those moments, I "sit on myself," and reward myself in my mind for having resisted the temptation.

"Sitting on yourself" is self-control. It is helpful in developing successful communications when you become aware of just how much guilt, blame and shame you put on people to try to get them to do what you want. It's sometimes difficult to stop this behavior when you've used it before to help you feel you are in control. Sit on yourself by not saying anything. Wait and watch the other person's ability to reason and think things through for himself.

We are a society of quick fixes and quick answers. We find it easy to do each other's work. Ironically, when we are honest with ourselves, we recognize that we could be doing whatever it is we're trying to get the other guy to do. AAhhhh, now there's some food for thought!

"How are you able to form these vessels
so that they possess such convincing beauty?"
"Oh," answers the potter,
"you are looking at the mere outward shape.
What I am forming lies within.
I am interested only in what remains
after the pot has been broken."
It is not the pots we are forming,
but ourselves.

—Centering, by M.C. Richards

7. Reverse your descriptions and labels.

ON A SHEET OF PAPER MAKE A LIST OF ALL THE messages you remember receiving as a child: Dumb, Stupid, Mr. or Ms. Smartypants, Retard, Incompetent, Ugly, Nuisance, Bother, Irresponsible, Undependable, Lazy, Good-For-Nothing, Bad, Nerd. Within this list, you will see some of the beliefs you have held about yourself over the years. It usually doesn't feel good to recall these. However, these messages need to be addressed. If you have some discomfort attached, they are still significant to you today.

Think for a moment how you describe children, adolescents and adults. What messages do you transfer to them with your thoughts and body language? How much of what you think about other people comes forth in what you actually say, and the manner in which you say it? Speaking is putting voice to thoughts. Most often, our thoughts are all that need to be addressed.

Try reversing the negative words that were used to describe you. Reverse the words you use to describe people with whom you want a different relationship. This clears the way for productive and meaningful communication. You will be amazed at the openings that will occur. These are new opportunities for being heard. Make a bunch of new labels, and watch what happens!

*The difference between greatness
and mediocrity
is often how an individual views a mistake ...*
—NELSON BOSWELL

8. Release resentments.

ON A PIECE OF PAPER, write down everything you resent about someone you feel "pushes your buttons." Everything! How you feel they have hurt you needs to be validated and understood from two perspectives: first, from your innermost pain, and second, from a place forward in time, looking back upon this situation with adult understanding.

Resentment and past hurts are the walls that remain standing between you and the person with whom you desire to interact. To let the walls come down, you need to get in touch with what you perceive built the wall in the first place. So, get to work, and see what it really looks like from the inside out.

Keep your head and your heart
going in the right direction
and you'll not have to worry about your feet.
—UNKNOWN

9. "*Cut to the chase*" – better known as "*Get to the point?*"

C ONFRONTATION CAN BE EASY, GENTLE, nurturing and supportive. It eases the discomfort to move directly *into* what it is that needs to be said or asked. This does not need to be done in an insensitive way. You don't have to blast the person with all your accusations. *And you don't have to be right!*

Sometimes, our own discomfort propels us into being overpowering or forceful. This strategy gives you permission to simply and gently say what it is you feel and think is the truth. It gives you permission to know what you know, think what you think and feel what you feel.

Call a spade a spade, and don't lose sight of that spade in the face of early denial. For example, I deal with denial by waiting for the other person to give me an opening in our conversation in which I can address the facts. If, after my second attempt, their denial is still pretty strong, I'll back off and let it go. The seeds are planted and they don't have to "get it" today. If, however, their denial is softening, I'll gently bring the conversation around to the issue one last time to see if they want to discuss it further.

*We have forty million reasons for failure,
but not a single excuse.*

—Rudyard Kipling

10. Don't ask "why".

ASKING "WHY" ENCOURAGES people to come up with excuses or justifications. It changes nothing about a person's responsibility. Asking "why" places a judgment on others, teaching them that somehow they are accountable to us and not to themselves. In this age of building self-esteem, it is understood that awareness must come from within. Accountability must be experienced internally.

If you want to help someone overcome a harmful behavior, you might ask, "So, what is going on for you?" Ask him about the feelings and thoughts that preceded the action. Find out *the other person's* perception of the situation. Empower him by having him tell you what his options are. Encourage others to become more and more in charge of their thoughts and feelings. Let them know they are not accountable for anyone but themselves. This is where self-esteem is strengthened.

Some theorists say you should not acknowledge any form of an excuse, but I still like to work with people to give some direction and examples on which to base their future decisions and actions. The question "Why?" only teaches people to give excuses, to place a judgment, and then to be done with it until it happens again. The question "What?" gives people a focus, direction, understanding and a consequence. "What?" teaches accountability and provides an opportunity to *visualize* what they would like to see themselves do the next time.

In the middle of difficulty
lies opportunity.
—ALBERT EINSTEIN

11. Stop! Stop! Stop!

HOW OFTEN WE FIND ourselves in the midst of a conflict, yet not really sure how we got there. There is no law that says you have to keep forging ahead until someone wins. You can put up your hands to signal a time-out and ask, "What's going on here that we are doing this?" When you stop the action, you can begin something new. Stopping gives you the opportunity to ask for another perception, and perception is the key to understanding what needs to happen next.

So stop. You wouldn't consciously go through a red light, would you? Well, when the discussion is heated and not going anywhere, the light is red!

The river flows a winding course to the sea.
We must be equally flexible
if we hope to reach our goals.

—Nelson Boswell

12. Wait!

CONTRARY TO POPULAR belief, you do not have to know it all. In fact, it is much easier to accept that you don't know it all. You don't have to presume anything. Wait to know what you need to know about a situation. Then you can allow the answers to reveal themselves to you in their own time. Do you know of anyone who has patience down to a fine art? If you do, ask him how he thinks and how he allows things to work themselves out.

Breathe! Taking a deep breath gives your body a chance to relax a little, which allows you to get your feet back on the ground. It's amazing what happens when you wait and let the other person figure it out for himself. When you wait and allow the ideas to come in without force, new creative ideas emerge.

Always bear in mind
that your own resolution to succeed
is more important than any other one thing.
—ABRAHAM LINCOLN

13. Show up!

MANY TIMES, IT'S EASIEST TO isolate. Maybe we think we're too inept to pull off a certain task. Some of the best times I've had were a result of pushing past my resistance to the new and *showing up* to try something different.

It was very frightening when I first started speaking to adults about my program. I saw my audience from a child's eyes and thought, "These people will hurt me if they disagree with anything I have to say." I found that when I met my fears with positive self-talk, reminding myself that we were all on the same side – the side of children – I relaxed and moved confidently into my presentations. All I did was bring myself back into the present moment, show up and share what I loved most in the world.....talking about children, adults and healing relationships.

Remember, it is human nature for the people in your life to want to support you. *Show up* and let them.

Everyone will experience the
consequences of his own acts.
If his acts are right,
he'll get good consequences;
if they're not,
he'll suffer for it.

—HARRY BROWNE

14. Own your 50%.

THIS STRATEGY WAS DESIGNED TO assist people who have discovered that they have a tendency toward being co-dependent. What is co-dependency? Co-dependency is trying to fill your innermost needs through outside approval. Sometimes this is done by trying to be all and do all for all people. It may be trying to carry a load of 120 percent for the entire world. It could be wondering why people don't appreciate all the hard work you do for them, yet questioning why they aren't doing any of it for themselves!

Co-dependency is reading self-help books for other people! Co-dependency is giving a self-help book to other people and telling them that the book was written just for them. Co-dependency is not understanding that the book is perfect for you! Doing people too many favors teaches them: one, you are a slave, or, two, they are simply too incompetent to do anything for themselves. So why should they bother when you'll do it for them?

Co-dependency is owning more than your 50 percent. It can be most helpful to know that you need only be 50 percent responsible for your interactions. You can relieve yourself of an enormous burden by understanding that people are capable of learning what they need to know and are capable of speaking for themselves. It is their responsibility to do so, or miss out!

In moving away from co-dependency, you will find that you need the other person to have a discussion. You will find that you don't have to know it all, and in some situations, you may even find *you don't know nuthin'!*

What the superior man seeks is in himself;
what the small man seeks is in others.
                    —FRANCOIS LA ROCHEFOUCAULD

15. Be 100% accountable.

AND YES, I AM ALWAYS 100 percent accountable for me. Oh, I can blame you for the things I feel you've done. Yet, what was I doing there with you? What was my 50 percent in the interaction with you in the first place? Yes, I am capable of taking care of myself. I am dependent on me for getting what I need or asking for it. No one can do this for me. If someone freely assists me along the way, then that's great. It is not their responsibility to take care of me. By the same token, if I desire to give of myself to another person, I am still 100 percent accountable for the gift that I offer without conditions. I am 100 percent accountable for all I say and do, whether I meant to or not! I am also 100 percent responsible for saying what I think and how I feel; no one can know that for me.

Doesn't this somehow make it all easier?

If a person continues to see only Giants,
it means he is still looking at the world
thru the eyes of a child.

—ANAIS NIN

16. *Look*

WHAT THE HECK is going on here, anyway? If you are in a heated argument, pay attention to what it looks like. Look to see if there is another perspective. If you are working with a child, look at the situation from a child's perspective. It seems that many adults today are working on their childhood issues. You might be well-advised to look at any heated situation from a child's perception. If your buttons are intensely pushed, it is a clear indication that something old and painful is coming up from the past. Take a new look at your situation, and see what it is that could be happening.

*The courage
to speak
must be matched
by the wisdom
to listen.*
                —UNKNOWN

17. LISTEN. "Laying on of ears."

THIS IS ONE OF the loveliest and most healing gifts we can possibly give. It comes from a place within us where there is no judgment, just love. It is listening to others—not thinking you should fix them or tell them what to do. It is wonderful for you as well to let go and be "in the moment." You will be amazed at the way listening can heal the most rebellious, defiant and resistant of people. So just listen. *Listen from your heart, and experience a new awareness.*

*Adventure is not outside a man,
but within.*

—Roy S. Baker

18. Do what's in front of you to do.

WHAT'S UP? IS THERE AN OPPORTUNITY that keeps knocking on your door? Well, why do you think it keeps coming? Sometimes you are not ready. After a while, you may start getting used to the idea, but still not do it! It is only fear of failure that holds us back and after all, failure is just an illusion we sometimes give our power away to.

My favorite rule of thumb is that if an idea presents itself to me three times, I will take a serious look at doing it. The idea for this book came to me three times and in three different ways. The first two times, I didn't really see how it was supposed to happen. By the third time, the idea was so concrete that I was fully aware of the opportunity it presented to me. I knew immediately how to do it and made a commitment to bring it about.

So go ahead right now and create the picture that you want. Be willing to do whatever it takes to make it happen! How many balls do we have to swing at before we hit a home run? It doesn't really matter if you will just keep your eye on the ball and continue to do what's in front of you to do. And remember, to get a home run, you have to meet the ball.

Nothing splendid has ever been achieved
except by those who dared believe
that something inside of them
was superior to circumstance.

—Bruce Barton

19. Less effort, more results.

M ANY PEOPLE WILL READ THIS AND SAY, "What? How can that be? Don't you realize you have to work hard to get places?"

I have a friend who built a multimillion dollar empire in only three years. Luck? No. He was just doing what was in front of him to do and applied this strategy in all business dealings.

Applying less effort allows for more results This may seem odd, yet it makes sense if you think about it. For example, what do you do when a pushy sales clerk pressures you to buy something? Chances are, you run the other way. Remember, too, that the creative flow of energy you need to pull together projects and opportunities can escape if you're exhausted from worry and trying to force things. "Efforting" is like spinning your wheels and getting nowhere fast.

Timing is the key to all success, not just in business, but in relationships as well. So whenever you find someone resistant to you, kick back, take a deep breath and say to yourself, "Less effort, more results." Invariably, your mind will receive new information, and you will be able to approach the problem in a different manner.

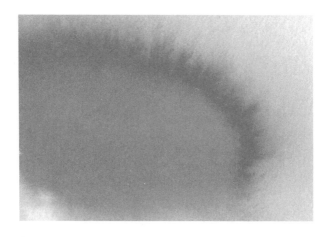

The more I surrender,
the more love I feel.
I'd rather feel love than win.
–Bob Mandell

20. Surrender.

THIS IS A STRATEGY THAT frightens many people. There is a misconception that "to surrender" means "to lose." You might want to ask yourself, "What is it I feel I will lose?" Maybe you have already lost it!

Surrender *simply* means letting your defenses down. It doesn't mean lie down and get stomped on; it just means "cool your jets," or yield.

Sometimes, we're so intent on being "right" that we dominate an interaction until it has no place to go. This can happen easily with children because we see them as *less than* or *not equal* to us.

When you find yourself not getting anywhere, think in terms of letting go a little. You've heard of surrendering to love? Well, when you let your guard down, you'll find that feelings soften and communications improve. Surrender doesn't mean "don't be safe"; it means "allow for a little openness and change."

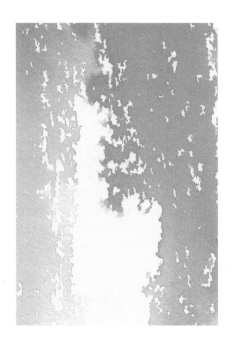

*One of the great keys to joy and happiness
and results in life is to develop the ability to
ask for what you want in such a manner
that people are delighted to give it to you.*

—Stuart Emery

21. *Ask*.

ASK FOR WHAT YOU WANT AND NEED. Get in touch with what it is you really want. Don't expect other people to read your mind. Take responsibility and ask for what you need from people. You don't have to be demanding, nor does one person have to give you exactly what you desire. Put your request out there for people to hear and to see. Keeping it a secret guarantees that it will not happen.

Ask, ask, and ask again. Ask to be heard when you are asking. Ask to know what's going on for someone who chooses not to give you what you feel you need. Learn to take some risks so you can understand how you are interacting with those whom you feel refuse your requests in some way. Ask yourself, "Have I been clear with them about what it is I need? Have I given them the complete picture? Have I made it a guessing game? Have I come off as demanding? Did I get angry with them when I thought they were refusing me instead of the request I was making? Were they supposed to read my mind?"

Ask.

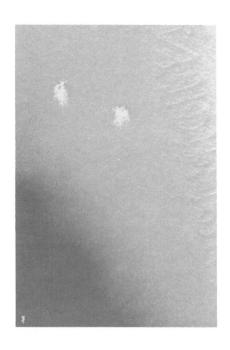

It's the song you sing and wear,
That makes the sun shine everywhere.
      —James Whitcomb Riley

22. Make a new label, paint a new picture, sing a new song.

IN LEARNING HOW TO REVERSE THE roles we have played and outgrown, we must first have a picture, or a *sense*, of what we want to be. It is necessary to create new labels for ourselves and the ways in which we choose to see others. Self-talk is the way we can replace negative chatter – those little gremlins inside our heads that try to convince us we shouldn't have what our hearts desire. We can chase those gremlins away with new labels and affirmations of what we want, desire and deserve. Do it now!

Research indicates that the more we deliberately impact the chatter in our heads with strong, positive statements, the greater our chances at success. Take some time to really hear the songs you listen to on the radio. Do they reinforce that your heart is always gonna get broken? Turn it off! Get some new music to support the new language you want to bombard your conscious mind and subconscious. *Get in touch* with a new picture. Paint pictures for other people. Pass it on.

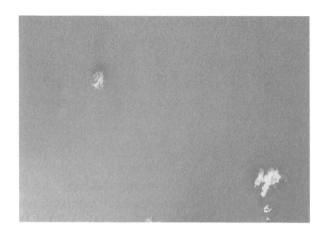

For every minute
you are angry,
you lose sixty seconds
of happiness.

—U<small>NKNOWN</small>

23. Rage reduction

THIS IS THE NEW FORM OF therapy being used to try to help children resolve the pain and anger associated with early abandonment issues. Anger is an emotion that can take us right through the red lights of life. You know the ones — the times when you say to yourself, "I knew better!" When anger builds up without some form of release, it can cause us to say things that are harmful to ourselves or others. If it is repressed, it can lead to physical discomfort and possibly illness.

One form of rage reduction could be a good old-fashioned "cry and carry-on spree!" You can get in your car, leaving it turned off and parked in the garage or in the nearest deserted street or parking lot, and then scream your pain away! Scream until the tears come. Tell it like it is, get to what you are really hurt about. Scream until it is gone — until that piece of work is done.

Louise Hay, author of *You Can Heal Your Life*, suggests beating your bed once a week whether it needs it or not. There is also "the hand-over mouth scream," coupled with stomping your feet. Both can be very effective in either helping you release your anger or making you feel so ridiculous that you will laugh! Another great form of release is to turn up the music in your car radio and sing at the top of your lungs. Whether you know the words or not, sing until you feel physically renewed.

Get rid of that built-up tension in a constructive way. Then you can talk to people about the issues at hand. Remember, it is "your" anger and deserves "your" attention! Learn to manage your emotions in ways that clear you out, not block you up. The benefits of releasing your pain will eventually help you pave a road to a greater understanding about "your" participation in the situations where you've felt victimized. You may begin to notice as you do this type of work that instead of feeling anger and pain, you begin choosing understanding first and release second.

You give but little
when you give of your possessions.
It is when you give of yourself
that you truly give.

—KAHLIL GIBRAN

24. Give away what you want.

IF YOU WANT LOVE, GIVE IT away. If you want respect, give it away. If you want honesty, be completely honest. If you want cooperation, be cooperative! Things will return to you in the same way you transmit them. Be aware of the words you use to describe people, whether or not they hear you directly. *What you speak travels.*

In relationships, we often find ourselves attached to an outcome. Give away what you want. This is the strongest strategy I have come across, for it reinforces unconditional giving. Allow and trust the gift of giving from the heart. You can expect the best for others – just don't attach yourself to what "the best" has to look like for them or for you. Release your gifts to them; let them do what they will.

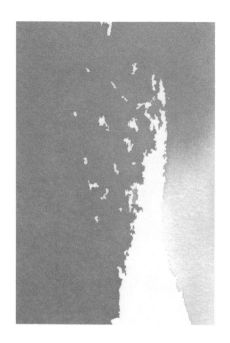

The indispensable first step
to getting the things you want out of life is this:
decide what you want.

—Ben Stein

25. Teach people how to treat you.

IF YOU FIND YOURSELF BECOMING a victim in business or in personal relationships, then you are teaching people it is all right to treat you in this fashion. This strategy doesn't mean attack back, for then you will be teaching people to attack you. It means learning to say "no" firmly, and being willing to do something different if you feel your requests have not been honored. If someone in your life is constantly bugging you, then the question to ask is, "How am I allowing this?"

The second question to ask yourself is, "What is it going to take to change this situation?" Once you've asked and answered these two crucial questions, you will be on your way to initiating new results by the ways you are now choosing to honor and represent yourself. If it doesn't appear to work the first time you try, then try, try again. Don't give up. This is *your* cycle we are talking about. Change takes time, patience, and perseverance.

*The whole of virtue
consists in its practice.*
—Cicero

26. Initiate integrity.

HOW DO YOU KNOW THAT integrity even matters? Initiate it, model it, and you will see how dramatically it comes back to you through other people and situations. When you find yourself in a situation that feels uncomfortable, simply refuse to participate. You can excuse yourself quietly, or you can voice your concern. Whichever way you choose, when you catch yourself dabbling with a negative, just stop yourself. You will have a greater sense of self-esteem each time you resist the temptation to harm someone with your words or actions. No matter how indirect or secret you think you are being, you will always know what you know deep inside. It will continue to affect your relationship with yourself and others. All you need do is inititate integrity, and it will have a ripple effect.

He who is most slow to a promise
is the most faithful in the performance of it.
—JEAN JACQUES ROUSSEAU

27. Commitment

HERE I QUOTE FROM A SEGMENT of W. H. Murray's writings. *Until one is committed, there is hesitancy, the chance to draw back, always ineffectiveness, concerning all acts of initiative (and creation). There is one elementary truth the ignorance of which kills countless ideas and splendid plans: that the moment one definitely commits oneself, then Providence moves too. All sorts of things occur to help one that would never otherwise have occurred. A whole stream of events issues from the decision, raising in one's favor all manner of unforeseen incidents and meetings and material assistance which no man could have dreamed would have come his way. I have learned a deep respect for one of Goethe's couplets:*

> *Whatever you can do,*
> *or dream you can, begin it.*
> *Boldness has genius,*
> *power and magic in it.*
> *BEGIN IT NOW.*

Love is unselfish,
understanding and kind,
for it sees with its heart
and not with its mind.
Love is the answer
that everyone seeks—
Love is the language
that every heart speaks.
Love can't be bought,
it is priceless and free . . .
Love, like pure magic,
is a sweet mystery.
                    —HELEN STEINER RICE

28. Stay in a loving space.

IN THE FACE OF CONFLICT, I FIND that staying in a loving space is a sure way to disengage myself from someone's anger, resistance, rebellion or confusion. I often use this in grocery stores and fast food chains, with my son's irritability, or with someone who is angry at me. It calms me down and reminds me that I want to come to a resolution in a peaceful manner.

My ability to stay calm and peaceful, while staying in a loving space, defuses and calms those around me. I keep breathing, I make sure both of my feet are on the ground and my arms are not crossed. I think loving thoughts and let negativity ricochet off me. Tai Chi is a form of defense in which a person under attack takes the energy and moves it off to the side, sending it away. What a lovely metaphor. Staying in a loving space keeps your defenses down and allows the other person to put voice to what it is he thinks is harming him. It opens the way to softer communication.

The secret of happiness is —
kindness,
seeing others as extensions
of one's own self.

      —UNKNOWN

29. *Reach out and touch someone*

THIS IS A SIMPLE STRATEGY, YET WE question ourselves — especially with children — as to whether or not we should touch or get physically close. Research indicates that we all need a certain amount of touching in our lives to stay alive. You can touch someone with your energy, smile, enthusiasm, support, listening and encouragement. It doesn't have to be physical. See yourself as touching lives in ways that are safe for you and in ways that honor others. What you give away is an immediate gift to yourself. You receive more when you give unconditionally.

This kind of reaching out and touching someone is like the feeling of giving a Christmas gift when you are full of that holiday spirit! Bring this feeling into every aspect of your life. Receive from yourself the acknowledgement you deserve for giving in the ways that you do. Own up to how wonderful you are. Give of yourself to other people. You are needed and wanted in this world. Reach out and touch someone so that it can come back to you in ways you never dreamed were possible.

*As in this lifetime there is one great
flowing process with a beginning, a middle
and an ending, so with our letters.
Start with the pen firmly on the paper,
pause a moment to feel where you are
and remain fully present
throughout the entire process.*

—FRANCES MANOLA

30. Write, write, write.

WRITING IS AN AGE-OLD METHOD OF COM-munication that facilitates clarity and feelings and has the potential to heal and open communication. Write to yourself. Write your parents a letter that begins, "Dear Mom and Dad, What I've always wanted to tell you is....." Get those feelings out one way or another. Send the letter or burn it.

When writing about the past, remember *you* are the one who is stuck in the time warp. While you are writing about something that happened in 1958, your parents are in the here and now. The most they can do for you is apologize. You will only cause more pain and separation if you use attack as a means to heal the past with them. You must do your own leg work to heal whatever was hurt deep inside of you. This task is for you; it's what builds your self-esteem and heals the cycles of failure that you carry into today. What matters is finishing the business of the past and bringing relationships up to date. Bringing your feelings to paper helps release them.

If you are an educator or parent, have your children keep a journal. Give them assignments to write about their feelings or thoughts in non-structured, as well as structured, formats. Write your children back. You will see a dramatic difference in their performance when you establish a relationship through writing.

The day you take complete
responsibility for yourself,
the day you stop making any excuses,
that's the day you start to the top.
                    —O.J. SIMPSON

31. Teach independence.

WHEN YOU ARE INDEPENDENT, YOUR sense of well-being is not contingent upon someone or something outside of yourself. Your very presence demonstrates a sense of self that is free from control or influence. You don't have trust issues with other people because you trust yourself to work through whatever arises on life's road. And you aren't dependent on other people to depend on you. It's that simple. It's not that it's easy, but it's that simple.

Confused? To some degree, we all have the need to be needed. It's what makes us feel significant and real in the world. We carry out our dependency needs with people to the same extent that they are returned to us. We may find we are trying to be responsible for someone else's life or problem. You may say, "I don't need those jerks relying on me every step of the way." Great. If this is what you want, let go now, and allow whatever happens to happen. Be independent and see what happens to those you once considered helpless or hopeless. Treat them as if they were fully competent to do for themselves by maintaining your own sense of freedom and competency.

"If you love someone, set them free," teaches us that independence is necessary in developing healthy, fulfilling relationships. This might bring up a fearful thought such as, "What if he makes it without me and doesn't need me anymore?" Being independent doesn't mean that you have to do everything entirely alone or that you won't matter to anyone anymore. It just means you can depend on yourself to find the right avenues to accomplish the success that you desire. *You are the only one responsible for how you experience your life.*

Wherever you are
it is your friends
who make your world.
—WILLIAM JAMES

32. Establish interdependence.

WHO ARE YOU? WITHOUT THE JOB, WITH-out the family, friends or financial status...who are you and what do you bring as your contribution to society and to yourself? Once you answer these questions and practice being in touch with who you are inside out, you offer interdependence within your work and personal relationships. What you bring to family, work and play is you! Interdependence breeds success for all who participate with a knowing of who they are.

Because we all need to be needed to some extent, it is necessary to be a part of a community, family or business. We weren't meant to do it all alone. This is how you get to give and how it is intended that you receive as well. Knowing who you are allows you the freedom and desire to give as well as receive. Because you know who you are, you understand that receiving is not only a gift to the person giving, but also that you are worthy of receiving. Worthiness is necessary to all success. You will probably not find total happiness doing it all alone. Success feels like success when we share it. Sharing our success encourages others to follow. Know that your success is a gift to all who know you. *You don't have to fail to get the support you need!*

The first great gift
we can bestow on others
is a good example.
　　　　　　　—THOMAS MORELL

33. Allow 10-17% dependence.

USE THIS PERCENTAGE AS a "guesstimate" when involving yourself with someone. To allow anything more might mean that you are becoming "selfless," and with that comes loss of self. Who's going to hold you up? You are, that's who. So watch yourself. Be giving, but don't work so hard at it. Allow the others in your life to do and think for themselves if you really want them to be well and happy.

Make time for yourself to read, meditate, think, ponder, create, rest or just be still. We are discovering that to allow excessive dependency enables a person to remain helpless. Cheering them on supports them to do their best. Expect the best for the people that you care about, and they will feel the possibility for themselves.

*Most people
are about as happy
as they make up
their minds to be.*
                —ABRAHAM LINCOLN

34. Withholding brings separation and pain.

THE EXERCISES IN NO. 8, *Releasing Resentments*, allows you to find out what situations you are holding onto emotionally. In holding onto resentment, we naturally withhold love, affection and regard for those we feel have harmed us or let us down. We do this to protect ourselves from future occurrences. By keeping our feelings in, we are not protecting ourselves. We are separating ourselves from those we love and care about. Someone has to make the first step forward, and it may as well be you if you are the one feeling the pain. Withholding keeps things in a miserable state. It is a game in which everybody stands to feel separation and pain longer than necessary.

Your only obligation
in any lifetime
is to be true to yourself.
                    –Richard Bach

35. Embracing brings acceptance.

IT IS DIFFICULT TO ADMIT THAT you have been misguided or wrong in some way. It brings up feelings from childhood of being "little-little," or "powerless." In understanding this, it is easier to accept quickly that you've made a mistake. Embracing yourself in these moments heals your innermost fear of not being good enough, or being child-like and powerless. Embrace yourself for being who you are.

Be gentle with that "little-little" boy or girl inside you who feels shamed for responding to the world in unskilled, unsophisticated or child-like ways. Embrace yourself, for you have just done what was familiar and what you believed would work. Accept that you can change anything about yourself that you want with patience, perseverance and gentle guidance. Embrace yourself and embrace others who are striving to heal their lives with the opportunities that life offers.

Blessed are they who have the gift
of making friends,
for it is one of God's best gifts.
It involves many things,
but above all,
the power of going out of one's self,
and appreciating whatever is noble
and loving in another.

—Thomas Hughes

36. Appreciation raises self-esteem, self-esteem increases productivity

When working with people who are experiencing low self-esteem, it is most healing to appreciate them just the way they are. Part of the problem with people who are underachieving, is their fear they will never measure up, so they don't try. When you acknowledge someone for just being here, it can make a world of difference in his level of productiveness.

In working with at-risk youth, it is necessary to build a relationship first and then encourage them to get down to work. Being productive builds self-esteem. It is amazing how a child acts when you say, "Johnny, I am really glad that you are here today and thank you for sharing what's going on for you. Now, it's time to get to work." And then see to it that Johnny gets to work. When he feels he may fail, say, "Yes, you can, yes, you can, yes, you can and I will support all efforts you choose to make." It is such a simple strategy, yet so powerful.

It often amazes me how quickly this strategy gets students up off their duffs and working beyond their usual pace. I listen carefully to their beliefs and perceptions about themselves, then I honor their fear that they are less than what they could be. After total acceptance of their feelings, I tell them that it's time to work and that I will support them. In a relatively short amount of time, relationship building, boundary setting and affirmations can be established, thus empowering them to be capable individuals.

One day a student had forgotten to take his medication. I was warned that this kid could get crazy without it. I made a decision to get *amnesia* and not ask him if he had taken it that morning. Instead, I inititated a relationship with him the minute he came in the room. We discussed several issues that were bothering him. Then he calmly went to work and turned in several assignments. It wasn't until later that afternoon that I found out from another teacher that he had not taken his medication, and to her surprise, he was doing very well!

Acknowledgement calms children, adolescents and adults. Acceptance heals innermost conflict, reduces fear of failure and heightens self-esteem. Make others feel that they matter. *Appreciation needs to be given unconditionally.*

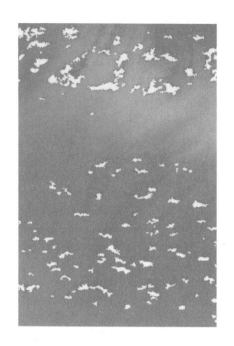

You can preach
a better sermon
with your life
than with your lips.
—GOLDSMITH

37. Reduce all nagging, complaining, and criticising to one minute or less.

THIS FOLLOWS SUIT WITH NO. 36. When we focus excessively on the negative, we ensure more of the same. How can anyone ever move beyond failure when the focus is on how he failed? Nagging builds negative chatter in the minds of those with whom we are venting our feelings. Is this what you want them to hear and remember you by? Is it any surprise that the people you nag choose not to remember what you said or want to be near you?

Think about it. What's it like being with you, anyway? What do you want them to hear inside their heads when they are making future decisions? How does this sound coming from the resources of your mind: "How many thousands of times do I have to tell you how to do this? What's the matter with you? Can't you think? Can't you read?" An alternative to this might be, "Johnny, I know that you can make a wise choice, next time. Johnny, you can do it, you can do it, I know you can do it."

*It is one of the most
beautiful compensations
of this life
that no man
can sincerely try to help another
without helping himself.*
—RALPH WALDO EMERSON

38. Get a life!

RESEARCH IN FAMILY DYNAMICS AND dysfunction indicates that the largest contributing factor to illness, disease and addiction is the result of a *loss of self*. Today, female and male roles are being redefined. Relationships are becoming more autonomous, with an emphasis on interdependency. This means we can no longer be obsessed about the people in our lives and remain healthy. It means that we must find our own expression in life, and not be dependent on someone else to provide this for us.

What is your dream? What is your specialty? Everyone has one and so do you. What do you do if you realize you don't have one yet? Get involved in your community, church, or service organizations. Network and build yourself a support system that extends beyond — yet can also include — your immediate family. The planet needs your participation. Your family needs you to be happy and fulfilled, not immersed in their lives. Healthy families breathe easily and support interdependence.

The people who get on in this world
are the people who get up
and look for the circumstances they want,
and, if they can't find them,
make them.

—GEORGE BERNARD SHAW

39. Use your imagination.

W HAT WOULD YOU HAVE YOUR life look like if it could be any way you wanted it? Your imagination is a key element in being able to see other possibilities for yourself, as well as for encouraging others. It is a gift and it is fun. Often we think things can only go one way – the way in which they have always gone. Imagination is the tool used to form all man-made inventions. You may be the next Thomas Edison or Albert Einstein.

Why don't we use our imagination? Again, it's an issue of knowing who we are and trusting our inner ability to figure out or know what to do in all of life's situations. Imagination leads you to who you are. Imagination gives you the ability to explore yourself and fulfill your dreams. All you have to do is loosen up and give yourself permission to use it any time you want to. Use it as a strategy for all future problem solving and resolution. Your imagination will show you the way when you remain open to it. Use it.

Treat people as if they were what they should be,
and you help them become
what they are capable of becoming.

–Johann Wolfgang von Goethe

40. See yourself or the person in question "as if" they already are successful.

WHEN WORKING WITH people who are challenging, this strategy allows for all levels of opening in human behavior and conditioning.

Over the years, the most success that I have experienced with children and adolescents comes from using this strategy. Regardless of the way they initially behaved or performed in my classroom, I continued to see them and treat them "as if" they could do absolutely everything I was asking of them. The outcome was that they did everything I required and more. Their test scores proved it, not only in their daily work, but on the Scholastic Aptitude Tests given at the end of each year. One year, my students' scores revealed an overall average of 2.5 years growth in my classroom. The norm for an average gain is 1 to 1.5 years growth per year.

This is a wonderful strategy to apply in your personal life as well. In becoming an author and public speaker, not only did I have to design my own path, I had to see myself walking it. I was nervous and anxious in preparing for engagements. I practiced seeing myself "as if" I were an already recognized author and speaker. It not only calmed me, but it also allowed me to feel fully present and professional during those early moments of a presentation.

Someone has to believe in you, and it helps to have supporters cheering you on. However, it all comes down to you who does the doing. You'll do yourself a great service by seeing yourself "as if." The sooner the better.

The lure of the distant and the difficult
is deceptive.
The great opportunity
is where you are.

—John Burroughs

41. *Release your attachments to the outcome.*

REDUCE YOUR EMOTIONAL drain: *detach, detach, detach!* When using your imagination and seeing yourself or someone else "as if," the key component to allowing these strategies to work effectively is to release your attachment to the outcome. It doesn't matter what road needs to be traveled to get you to where you are going. All that matters is that you get there. So, see it, act "as if" it has been achieved already, and release your hold on the situation or the people involved. Remember, less effort, more results. This is the key to healthy relationships and productive situations. You empower yourself and other individuals when you allow them to determine their own outcomes, just as you would expect to be free to experience your own.

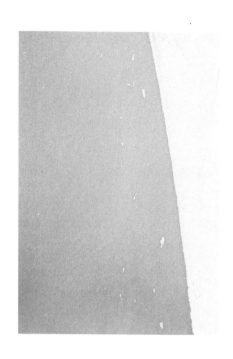

I love you
no matter what.
I will love you
if you are stupid,
if you slip and fall on your face,
if you do the wrong thing,
if you make mistakes,
if you behave like a human being –
I will love you no matter.

–LEO BUSCAGLIA

42. Discipline with love, logic and firmness.

*C*HILDREN ARE CRYING OUT for love. Many adults are, too. Love is best demonstrated by loving discipline, by saying, *"No, you cannot.* This is potentially harmful, and I love you too much to allow you to hurt yourself." This lesson teaches that rules exist to keep everyone safe. Following up on a rule is sometimes very uncomfortable for the adult. Often, it might be easier to let it slide.

If you really love someone, you will teach him he is worth the effort by keeping him safe and insisting that he act appropriately. Being firm and fair shows the depths of your love and concern. It's difficult to rebel when someone is tender and expressing deep feelings, while telling you that what you want to do will not be allowed because it is not safe or appropriate.

It is a funny thing about life;
if you refuse to accept anything but the best,
you very often get it.

—SOMERSET MAUGHAM

43. Expect the BEST.

EXPECT IT. DEMAND IT. In our society, we often underestimate human potential because we feel sorry for the young people coming to us from disastrous home situations. Each time we accept a child's home situation as disabling the child, we are disabling the child as well.

One year I had a partially deaf and blind boy, Thomas, in my class. In his previous year, Thomas got to go home two or three times a week. He spent as much time as he could in the special education room. He was often excused from school because his tolerance level was low, and he became disruptive in the classroom.

Thomas came into my classroom that fall looking and acting pretty crazy. I told him he couldn't act crazy anymore, period! I backed it up with expecting the best and telling him so. He stopped acting crazy within a few short weeks and by the end of the year, he didn't even want to go to special education classes anymore. He was so involved in our classroom projects that he didn't want to miss out. The children in the classroom treated him as one of them, because I did.

Six years later, Thomas graduated from high school with a scholarship to a community college. I almost didn't recognize his senior picture because he looked incredibly sane, confident and handsome.

Expect the best of all people, regardless of the appearance of any disability. Expecting the best will have a ripple effect in all that goes on in your personal and professional relationships.

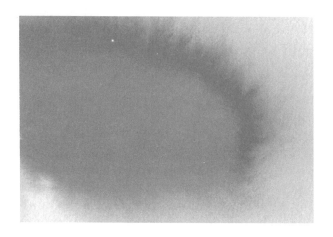

The object of teaching a child
is to enable him
to get along
without his teacher.

—Unknown

44. Teach boundaries, allow boundaries, have boundaries.

A BOUNDARY IS AN INVISIBLE SPHERE you need to have around yourself to stay safe from unwanted intrusion, interruption or absorption. It was once a common misbelief that we should never have boundaries in love. It is now understood that boundaries teach love — love of self. Love of self develops and increases self-esteem and self-worth. Being "self-less" can empty your cup. When you have an empty cup, there is nothing left to give. It is important to give to yourself first, keeping your cup well taken care of, in order to be of service to others.

Boundaries teach love. Giving a child boundaries demonstrates love. It shows the child that you care enough to see to it that he is always safe and cared for. Children need to experience this. Adults need to feel this with you as well. Establishing boundaries with adults teaches them that *you* love yourself enough to remain safe, thus reducing the likelihood of victimization. It provides an increased trust and sensitivity in communication for all involved. Teach love. Provide boundaries.

Opportunity...
Often it comes disguised in the form of misfortune,
or temporary defeat.

—Napoleon Hill

45. There are always two options!

IN TEACHING ACCOUNTABILITY, it is necessary to provide opportunities in which there can be "scientific experimentation." These experiments are often intended to challenge any new rule you may have set for someone. Accept their attempts as trial and error. To help people become accountable and responsible for their behavior, allow them their failure and provide them with two options. They can either do it within the boundaries that you've established, or they can do it their way and take consequences for "choosing" to disregard your request.

It's really as simple as that, as long as you see to it that the consequences are enforced. Allow them the opportunity to grow. Reduce your emotional drain by delighting in their attempts to see if rules really do apply to them. Have fun with this. Acknowledge them and accept their need to challenge the new.

Everybody thinks of changing humanity
and nobody thinks of changing himself.
—LEO TOLSTOI

46. Before you can change anyone else, you must first change yourself.

*P*UT A STAR BY THIS ONE. THIS IS THE strongest and most powerful strategy I have come across. I don't always like it because I'd really rather the other person do the changing. At those times when nothing I've tried has worked with a person, I stop and remember this strategy. It often aggravates me as I know it will work when I apply it. I have to be willing to see things from a new perspective in order to see it work. It generally has to do with an aspect of my attitude that I don't want to surrender or give up about someone.

I'd much rather have something "on" somone else than admit that I was wrong in some way. So, I sometimes go into this strategy stomping my feet and grumbling in my head. Yet when I get honest with myself, I realize that I have a negative attitude about them. They may have felt this from the way I've interacted with them, even though I've done my best to hide it from them and myself. They resisted working with me at a level which I wanted. Why wouldn't they? After all, I'm the one with an attitude!

Oh, yes, they might have an attitude about me as well, and I'll have to let that go too if I have any hopes of getting along with this person. The real magic is that their attitude about me changes almost instantaneously as a result of my changing my thinking. You don't have to believe this works, just try it as honestly as you can and see what happens!

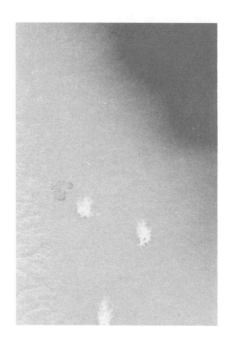

What we are looking for
is that which is looking.

47. Check your mirror!

MIRRORING IS PROBABLY THE oldest known self-correcting strategy known to man. It coincides with NO. 25, *Teach people how to treat you,* and goes even deeper into what it is we are projecting. Children are a perfect example of this. Whether you are their parent or classroom teacher, children can reflect different aspects of your personality back to you. Sometimes we don't like what we see. At these moments it can be to our benefit to be as honest as we can about what we are projecting in this relationship.

Mirroring does not mean that I am exactly like someone else. It is only an indicator of something past or present. It may show me a personal characteristic I am uncomfortable with and choose not to be a component of my nature. Those closest to us can reflect our innermost attitudes and beliefs. It is my responsibility to determine if I like what I see. If I don't, then it is up to me to seek ways to change that which I no longer desire to have as an aspect of my character.

It is in men
as in sails
where sometimes
there is a vein of gold
which the owner
knows not of.
                    —Jonathan Swift

48. See yourself as an opportunity seeker.

KEEP YOUR EYES AND MIND open. When you are developing success, it is important to see that opportunity is constantly extending itself to you in many ways. Sometimes we may see a "challenging" person as a nuisance. This person is only providing us with a variety of opportunities to figure out what needs to be changed. Many times, we will try to shove opportunity aside instead of facing it head-on. This could be why it keeps coming to us again and again.

I once caught a third-grade girl hiding from me on top of a toliet in the girls' restroom. I opened the door and she looked as if I was going to chew her out. Instead, I seized the opportunity to prove to her that I would honor her resistance to me and not overpower her. I calmly and quietly handed her the note I had intended to give her before she darted into the restroom to avoid me. I closed the door and went on my way.

The next day she showed up at my office ready to do some counseling. This was an opportunity I could have let pass. It challenged me to win her confidence and trust in this way. I had needed something to get my foot in the door with her, and this opportunity proved perfect. It acknowledged and established boundaries in the early stages of building a relationship with a very resistive, angry young girl who was responding with fear, not defiance.

*History has demonstrated
that the most notable winners
usually encountered
heartbreaking obstacles
before they triumphed.
They won
because they refused
to become discouraged
by their defeats.*

—B.C. FORBES

49. REFUSE to accept the negative.

PUT ANOTHER STAR BY THIS ONE. We live in changing times. With this change has come skepticism and criticism. Refuse to hear it or to accept the negative. Refuse to believe the negative has to be the dominant aspect of a situation. *Refuse, refuse, refuse* to let negativity and self-imposed limitation take root in your thinking. Refuse to accept the negative aspects of others as the only truth about them. See beyond the small picture.

Maybe there's a silver lining behind every dark cloud, and maybe there isn't. If you choose to believe there can be, then that will be your experience. Not all people like this idea, for it is far easier to bemoan the fact that life is full of suffering. Yet observe those people who seem to radiate happiness and health. They will tell you they refuse to get bogged down by the negative aspects that life can and sometimes does offer. They will tell you it is worth it to see a ray of light in those moments that appear to be the darkest. They will tell you life is meant to be lived.

When we work with children, adolescents or adults who come from negative home situations, we do them a great disservice if we attend only to their negative drama. We assist them in creating more failure or crisis if we don't empower them to see other alternatives. So refuse, resist, deny the negative. Try to shed some light on a negative situation. This is a strategy that opens the possiblity of another way of living life on the upswing, for yourself, and for all who come in contact with you.

When you follow your bliss,
you put yourself on a kind of track
that has been there all the while —
waiting for you.
And the life that you ought to be living
is the one you are living.
Wherever you are —
if you are following your bliss
you are enjoying that refreshment —
that life within you —
all the time.

—JOSEPH CAMPBELL

50. Extend your reach, extend your capability.

SOMETIMES YOU'VE JUST GOT TO GO THE extra mile. That's all there is to it. We all need to stretch ourselves from time to time just to feel that we are alive. This is not to say that life needs to be a crisis. Quite the contrary. It means that we are really committed to whatever it takes to accomplish what it is we desire, either for ourselves, or for the health and well-being of another person.

Sometimes, it means trying something new, challenging the old ways of thinking and being in the world. Sometimes, it means getting right out there on your growing edge and challenging yourself from the depths of your being. It may mean a change in career, or asking for an advancement with more responsiblity. It may mean attending to a relationship that you've previously taken for granted. It may mean allowing a new level of intimacy and vulnerability to evolve in the way you choose to be with yourself and those you care about.

It's definitely a stretch to make a decision to extend yourself in new and challenging ways. So go for it, and let it be fun and exciting.

Those who bring
sunshine to the
lives of others
CANNOT
KEEP IT FROM
THEMSELVES.
—James Barrie

51. Embrace success, own it, wear it, model it for others to see and affirm for you.

WITH NEWLY aquired success comes second guessing, sabotaging, fear, possibly more failure, trial/error and more attempts! Success comes by degrees so that we can get used to the idea and practice a new way of being in the world. Often, once some success has been achieved, we become impatient with ourselves or with others when we think it will not continue. It is very crucial, in building self-esteem and increasing the levels of success, to validate yourself and others for all attempts made along the way. Embrace it, receive it, model it and enjoy.

Lord, make me an instrument
of thy peace.
Where there is hatred,
let me sow love;
Where there is injury, pardon;
Where there is doubt, faith;
Where there is despair, hope;
Where there is darkness, light;
Where there is sadness, joy.
O Divine Master,
grant that I may not so much seek
To be understood,
as to understand,
To be loved, as to love.
For it is in giving that we receive,
It is in pardoning that
we are pardoned,
It is in dying to self
that we are born to eternal life."
—St. Francis of Assisi

52. Use words that heal.

WHATEVER HAPPENED TO BEING nice? I remember when I'd come to my mother complaining that the other kids were being mean. She would tell me to just be nice. I thought I was being nice! We reap the results of our efforts, therefore, I must not have been as nice as I thought I had been. The children were providing me with excellent opportunities to put myself back in *my* driver's seat by being nice. Using nice words defeats the intent of a negative and lifts you up and out of the victim position. It is taking your power back, and then expressing an inner caring, which can outweigh the pain and confusion someone may be directing at you.

It didn't make sense to me when my mother told me to be nice. I have found most children and even some adults have a difficult time understanding how this works. It would seem to some that attacking someone back would be what the other person *deserved*. How often in our own anger and disappointment we try to get back at the world for our pain? This only brings more separation and pain to both parties involved.

Being nice means choosing words that reflect gentleness and caring. Words heal. I have found that using words which transmit kindness and love dismantles the anger and pain. Use words that heal, that touch another person's inner self, the place where all goodness comes. Watch how words and acknowledgement heal, in times of joy as well as challenge. The words you use and the tone of your voice can be very calming and nurturing to people. It is a gift of human caring that you receive as well when you extend words that heal.

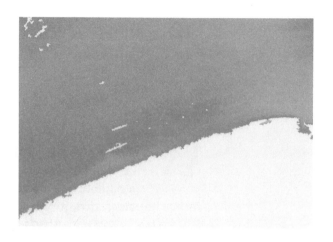

The first peace,
which is the most important,
is that which comes
within the souls of people
when they realize their relationship,
their oneness,
with the universe and all its powers,
and when they realize
that at the center of the universe
dwells the Great Spirit,
and that this center
is really everywhere,
it is within each of us."

—BLACK ELK

53. Turn it over to a higher power, quicker, soon, faster;

WHEN YOU BECOME AWARE that you have overextended yourself on a problem, and it all seems rather hopeless, turn it over and let it go. "Hopeless" is not such a bad place to be as you are developing and strengthening a sense of your own capabilities in the world. It is at this place that we can do nothing more than to trust something greater than ourselves. You've done your part. You've done the best that you can. It's out of your hands now anyway, and probably has been for quite some time. You were the only one who didn't get it!

So take a deep breath and remember who you are. You are a wonderful, loving, caring person who tried the best you could. Your relationship with a higher source will give you the freedom to move in new and creative directions, if you will ask for help, strength and guidance. The Twelve Step programs are based in this principle. It's worth considering? Yes!

Simplicity in all things
is the secret of the wilderness,
and one of its most valuable lessons.
It is what we leave behind
that is important.
I think the matter of simplicity
goes further than just food,
equipment and unnecessary gadgets;
it goes into the matter of thoughts
and objectives as well.
When in the wilds,
we must not carry our problems with us
or the joy is lost.

–SIGURD OLSON

54. K.I.S.S.

KEEP IT SIMPLE, SWEETIE! GET BACK to what is important, back to the basics; love, peace and human kindness. Slow yourself down. Every time I get behind a semitruck on the freeway, and it is impossible to get around I begin to feel my agitation increase. The agitation is an excellent reminder that I need to slow it down, take it easy, and know that things have a way of working themselves out. It's far more important that I "arrive" in life, than not get there at all.

So simplify your life. Trust that you can be alone with yourself and feel good. Trust that slowing down and allowing simplicity to seep in creates openings and an easy flowing existence. Know that there is an answer to all questions and that all problems eventually get resolved. Trust the beauty that life has to offer you by allowing simplicity into your life. Remember, making things too complicated and hurried risks success. Slow down, love yourself, love life and love being in the present moment.

*Success doesn't come to you . . .
you go to it.*

—MARVA COLLINS

55. Get off it!

WHEN IS ENOUGH, ENOUGH? What's your bottom line? What's it going to take before you decide you have to be the one to do something different? Make the break, say what you need, visualize it and go after it. They say, *the pain is necessary and suffering is optional!*

Maybe it's just time for you to enjoy life. Maybe the failure wasn't really failure after all. Maybe it was just a state of mind that got you up off your duff, to see to it you get what you want and inherently deserve. Maybe you've pursued your dream and it didn't work out. Maybe you've worked on getting another person healthy and he just keeps sliding back. Get off it! The greatest gift you can give yourself and those who are in your life is to get on with it. Your happiness teaches happiness. Happiness is contagious...give it away! Remember, suffering is optional!

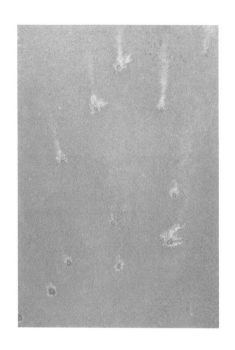

LAUGHTER
is the tranquilizer
with no side effects.
—ARNOLD GLASOW

56. See the humor, have a laugh, give up and smile!

THIS IS JUST EARTH SCHOOL, YOU KNOW. *Don't take your life personally.* I still don't know if I fully "get it," but I'm trying. Being human, ahhh, what an incredible task when most of us are perfectionists in some way. Yet, it is only through our humanness that love really seems to radiate from us. One year, at the end of my presentation, I was being my fully animated self when I swung my right arm forward and said, "...and so, it's time to take ACTION," and at that exact moment, I hit my glass of water and it shot half way across the room. This accident was perfect!

What if all mistakes were really on purpose, or what if there were no accidents? We'd all be alot more relaxed about things, and we'd just know that somehow this was all just to help us remember that we are only human after all! So see the humor as quickly as you can. Let the light into your laughter as you find yourself becoming more fully aware of your own presence and the presence of those around you.

Few things are impossible
to diligence and skill . . . . .
Great works are performed not by strength,
but of perseverance.

—SAMUEL JOHNSON

57. Nevertheless.

ARE YOU EXHAUSTED WITH THE CON-
stant complaints and resistance to
whatever it is you are asking to be done? My
son has his own ideas about how he would like
things to be, and I have mine. Without
overpowering him, I first try to really listen to
him when he doesn't want to do things my way,
such as obey a boundary I am establishing. I
listen and then say, "I understand that you
would rather do this another way, *nevertheless*,
I am the mom and I am the one who expects you
to follow through with what I've asked." If he
still chooses not to comply, he is then given two
options.

Nevertheless establishes that you've heard
someone's differing opinions, that it's O.K. to have
a different view, and that you've acknowledged
them and stated that their desires do matter.
Nevertheless is a long word for "however". It
reduces the drama of resistance in children and
adolescents. There is something about long words
that captures a child's attention and lets him know
you still mean business!

Success is failure turned inside out,
The silver tint of the clouds of doubt,
And you never can tell how close you are,
It may be near when it seems so far.
So stick to the fight when you're hardest hit,
It's when things seem worse,
That you must not quit.

—Unknown

58. Going through the "red lights" of life.

IF YOU FIND THAT YOU ARE DOING THINGS that you know better than to do, like actually driving your car through a red light even though you know it's dangerous, then you probably have too much "stuff" on your mind. If you find yourself jumping into situations that you know perfectly well you have no business being in, then you might be at a place called, "I need help."

If, after implementing each and every one of these strategies, you still find yourself in conflict, confusion or pain, you may want to look into doing what is now known as "inner work." There no longer appears to be the societal stigma on seeking professional help there once was. Now much of our society is seeking help beyond the family or work situation.

Therefore, if you have a cycle that keeps repeating itself, regardless of all that you have tried, or if you have excessive concerns about someone else, maybe it's time you asked for what you needed. It is human nature to need help in figuring out what's going on for us in this life. If your leg were broken, you wouldn't hesitate to get to the doctor, would you?

Many people have said to me that they either don't have the money or they don't see how a trained professional can tell them anything they don't already know. And I simply ask, "If your leg looked and felt like it was broken, what would you do?" Maybe, we initially tend to view therapy more like cancer; if you don't go to the doctor, you don't have to know whether you are going to die or not!

However, the largest percentage of responses I hear from people who have done "inner work" with trained professionals have been most positive. They affirm that it helped them immensely in turning their circumstances around. It is imperative that you find out how valuable and wonderful you really are. In working with a therapist you will receive tools that support you in creating your own success.

This is your life, and if it is broken and spellbound by failure, then it is up to you to get what support, focus and encouragement you need to make your life work. You deserve to be and have all that you desire. So take heart, start putting yourself first and do the work. You are the only you you'll ever have.

Each time you are honest
and conduct yourself with honesty,
a success force will drive you
toward greater success.
Each time you lie, even with a little white lie,
there are strong forces
pushing you toward failure.

—JOSEPH SUGARMAN

59. Tell the truth quicker, sooner and faster.

T RUTH CREATES INTIMACY WITH THE self. To experience intimacy with others, we must first learn to be intimate with ourselves. When facing our own denial, we clean out the closet. This gets pretty darn close to home as well as to the heart of significant issues within our lives. Getting honest is what allows an inner intimacy to become established within our character. Inner intimacy transmits a deep and solid respect for ourselves and others.

Stop underestimating the other person's potential for dealing with the truth. This is better known as enabling or controlling, which serves no one. We are often dishonest to avoid conflict or abandonment. This avoidance has everything to do with our beliefs that we are somehow less than the person we feel we must answer to. If we've been mistreated in the past as a result of being truthful, we may use white lies as a way to avoid dealing directly, and as an equal, with someone we are allowing to ride shotgun on us.

In taking a risk with truth, it might also be appropriate with some people to say, "This is the way it is and I'm sorry if this affects how you feel, however, this was the best I could do at the time." In saying this to people, especially those who you've experienced as abrasive in the face of truth, not only are they surprised with your refusal to be a victim, but they may also relax and become more willing to hear your feelings.

Another kind of truth that we can mistake as truth is really criticism. Sometimes we use truth as a means to control what someone else does, saying something like, "Well, I just thought you should know what other people are thinking and saying about you when you do these things to me." This is harmful and questionable as to whether it can even qualify as truth when used to discount, control or demoralize another human being. Truth is truth is truth. And if you haven't been asked for an opinion, don't feel it your duty to give it in the name of truth.

Truth increases intimacy and therefore has within it the potential to deepen success in work, play and significant relationships. It can be a genuine expression about the human experience as it is, not as someone else thinks it ought to be. Truth is first and foremost for you. Of course you can try to squeak by with less than total honesty. However, you still know what you know deep down inside. Honesty enhances and strengthens self-esteem, self-worth and self-value. So take a look at those little white lies and see if you can't own more of who you really are and take a few risks with eliminating them one by one.

*Finish each day and
be done with it.
You have done what
you could.
Some blunders and
absurdities no doubt creep in.
Forget them as soon
as you can.
Tomorrow is a new day.
You shall begin it
well and serenely.*
—RALPH WALDO EMERSON

60. Sleep on it ⟶!

ONE NIGHT I CALLED MY DAD, TOTALLY exhausted with the worries of the world on my shoulders. It was probably the first time I had ever shared my true feelings of helplessness with him, and he tried to console me. All he did that night was rally to my side and tell me it would be all right. This was exactly what I needed: my dad's approval and "knowing" that I could once again make everything all right in my life. At the end of our conversation, he told me to "*go sleep on it*" – that it would be better in the morning!

My parents were farmers and I realized that there had been many times that they had needed to do this exact same thing. I trusted the wisdom behind this suggestion. I put myself to bed after we finished our conversation. I cried myself to sleep, and chose to believe everything would look better in the morning. When I awoke, I did feel better. Shortly thereafter, I was able to find a new direction for myself as my feet were firmly back on the ground.

So, take a load off of yourself and put your problems down for at least one evening. Sleep, sleep, sleep on it and allow the answers to reveal themselves to you.

If I speak in the tongues of men and of angels,
but have not love,
I am a noisy gong or clanging cymbal.
And if I have prophetic powers,
and understand all mysteries
and all knowledge, and if I have all faith,
so as to move mountains, but have not love,
I am nothing.
Love is patient and kind;
love is not boastful; it is not arrogant or rude.
Love does not insist on its own way;
it is not irritable or resentful;
it does not rejoice at wrong,
but rejoices in the right.
Love bears all things, believes all things,
hopes all things, endures all things.
So faith, hope, love abide, these three;
but the greatest of these
is love.

—FIRST CORINTHIANS 13

61. Forgiveness, release & putting love first.

THIS STRATEGY, IN AND OF ITSELF, can bring you enough success to last a lifetime. Each time you find yourself stressed and self-absorbed with fear of not being good enough or less than, remember that the people who are frightening you are just wearing a protective coat of armor. The original intention of the armor was to defend them in the ways that they believed would keep them safe. That's all.

This strategy can help you understand that the attacks people sometimes make are done in the exact same fashion that they received as children. When you see an adult ridiculing or invalidating a child or another adult, quickly move into an understanding that this is a reflection of how they were treated as children. You can immediately see the inner child behind that rough exterior. How you approach this situation, as a result of your new perception, may transmit a message such as, *I'm on your side,* instead of, *I'll show you who can play tough ball!*

In putting love first, you will find that the weapons come down and the steel armor begins to melt. Your ability to *forgive* increases as you move into an understanding of this person's bigger picture of past trauma, separation and pain. In *releasing* judgement about this person's actions, you can more readily return to putting love first before you do or say anything further.

Good luck and peace be with you....

M ary Robinson, M.S. educational psychologist, family and child counselor, author, consultant, motivational speaker in the United States and Canada, and single parent, is recognized in educational communities for a program she developed as a result of extensive experience with at-risk youth and adults in crisis. Her program has assisted parents, educators and helping professionals with student attrition. She addresses the needs of adults as well as children in her trainings, seminars and workshops. Mary is known for her ability to "zero-in" on major issues, her professionalism, imagination, loyalty, strong work ethic, good sense of humor and play.

For current workshops, lectures, seminar schedules and other information, please contact:

Heart Publishing & Productions, (503) 771-9917 or 1-800-777-5458.

The Chinese symbol for "heart."

Order Form

Please send the following postpaid:

____YOU ARE A SUCCESS!
      61 Proven Strategies for Developing Success
                                  @ $14.95
____Root Yourself in Success --
      Poster with 61 Proven Strategies @ $15.00
____Package of 4 Bookmarks for Success @ $ 3.95
____Makin' Magic I --
      Eight Steps to Success Booklet @ $ 4.95
____Makin' Magic II --
      Ten Tricks That Work
        With At-Risk Kids! Booklet @ $ 4.95
____Makin' Magic III --
      Increasing Emotional Energy With
      At-Risk Youth — 90 min. video @ $69.95

Name_____

Address_____

City_____State_____Zip_____

Group discounts available. For more information call;
HEART PUBLISHING & PRODUCTIONS
P.O. Box 82037 • Portland, OR 97282
(503) 771-9917
FAX(503) 774-4457
1-800-777-5458